Your Drean

Twenty-First-Cent

Bonding

by

Darla Birde

♫♫♫

Discover one of the world's most captivating small pet birds...

This complete twenty-first-century guide will give you everything you need to get started with lovebirds, one of the world's most popular pet birds. Even if you're a complete beginner, this compact but complete book will give you the tools you need to get started right.

Want a single pocket pet? This book will explain why it is mission critical to begin with a young, healthy, hand-raised lovebird. And it will teach you what all bird owners should know to choose, bond with, and care for your perfect pet lovebird.

1

Want to keep aviary birds for their beauty? Want to explore the mysteries of breeding them for their wide variety of color mutations? This book, while not an exhaustive guide to breeding and hand-feeding love-birds, will give you a taste of what's involved and allow you to decide if you're ready to take your hobby further.

Copyright & Legal Note

I've made every effort to ensure that the information in this book was correct, but a book is never a substitute for your good judgment or the good

judgment of an avian vet. If your bird is sick, don't wait. Contact an emergency vet for help right now. For the record, I *never* assume any liability to any reader for any loss, damage, or disruption caused by an error or an omission in this book, regardless of the cause of the error or omission, including accidents, negligence, or acts of God.

Please Note: It is a violation of international copyright law to post this book to free or sharing sites.

Table of Contents

How Lovebirds Stole Our Hearts

THE FIRST LOVEBIRDS attracted human attention because of their boldness, their beauty, and their fierce devotion to their partners. The legend of the lovebird is the story of two small birds, tightly bonded together against the world. They became famous for their desire to go two by two— and their fierceness in defending their homes against other, much larger birds.

Because they bonded so fiercely with each other, they were not regarded as pets in the sense that a budgerigar or a cockatiel was regarded as a pet. Instead, they were regarded in a similar light to certain finches— as fine specimens that showed well in the show cage or the aviary.

Then came the rise of good hand-feeding tools and diets. For the first time, humans could raise baby lovebirds from an early age and transfer that fierce bond from another lovebird to their human companion.

Notice I don't say, "owner." As the companion of a lovebird, you are an "owner" only in the same sense that a cat "owner" is an "owner." These birds do have a mind of their own. Yet the challenges can make it even more meaningful when you succeed in winning the one-on-one devotion of your very own lovebird.

But, of course, there are lots of bold and beautiful pair-bond bird species in the world. Lovebirds maintain their enduring popularity because they offer several other advantages in addition to their beauty and their boldness.

*Lovebirds, especially the popular peach-faced lovebird, are easy to feed. They don't demand complicated diets, because they evolved to seek out seeding grasses.

*Lovebirds are hardy birds that offer trouble-free exotic colors instead of being hothouse beauties who demand a lot of fussing.

*Lovebirds are eager to breed when food, water, and a safe nesting site become available. In their natural environment, they must hurry to take advantage of the breeding opportunity when the rainy season comes. These adaptable birds turned out to be great candidates for hobbyists who wanted to develop a whole rainbow of color mutations.

When you add up these advantages, it makes sense that lovebirds were always destined to become a popular favorite.

In fact, one species, the peach-faced lovebird, is probably one of the top three most popular pet parrots kept in the entire world. The only parrots more commonly kept in captivity are the budgerigar (often called the parakeet in the United States) and the cockatiel.

In particular, lovebirds offer several advantages to first-time pet owners.

*Easy to feed on widely available, inexpensive food. With a few updates to the old-fashioned diets, your lovebird has a life expectancy of fifteen years or even longer.

*Once considered a hands-off bird, the rise of breeders who hand-feed baby peach-faced lovebirds means that these birds make a fine apartment pet for people who don't have the space or budget for a larger parrot.

*There is a strong hobby to support breeders who would like to learn to show prize birds and/or create beautiful mutations.

*Busy lovebird owners can keep a pair to create beauty and life in the home without a great deal of hands-on effort.

Before You Choose A Lovebird

LOVEBIRDS HAVE A LIFE expectancy of around fifteen years. Many birds, especially individual non-breeding pets, live much longer. I am aware of several people who claim that their still-living lovebirds are in their mid-twenties.

You and your family will be spending a considerable percentage of your life with your new lovebird, especially if you get your bird as a young hand-fed baby. Therefore, you want to think carefully before you bring your new bird home. Is this really the right pet for you?

Consider the following issues.

Does anyone in the home have asthma or allergies?

LOVEBIRDS AREN'T ONE of the species like cockatoos, lovebirds, or African greys who produce a great deal of dust. However, since it wouldn't be fair to bond with a new baby only to be forced to give it up, always check with your allergist before you adopt a new pet.

Do you really want a talking bird?

LOVEBIRDS AREN'T THE most talented talkers going. While some owners do claim to have talking birds, you'll find the voice tends to be high-pitched, shrill, and/or unclear. If you really have your heart set on a pocket-sized talking bird, you should consider a budgerigar instead.

Do you have enough time to spend

with your bird?

IF YOU PLAN TO ADOPT a solo hand-fed baby and keep the bird tame, you should plan on spending a lot of time with your bird each day. Lovebirds are pair-bond birds, and they are extremely devoted to their other half. People who work at home or in offices where they can spend hours in sight of their lovebird will have the happiest pets.

You should adopt at a time in your life when you have plenty of hours to spend bonding with your new lovebird. You really can't put it off. The lovebird brain tends to get very set in its ways. If the baby is not tamed and trained young, you will have a great deal of trouble ever taming and training the bird at all.

Because of the psychology of the pair-bond, a single lovebird can't live as a pretty flower expected to make a fine show in a cage. A single bird wants to come out, maybe sit on your shoulder or computer or scramble around on your curtains or a birdie playpen. Your pet will be curious about your activities and want to get involved. Don't be surprised if a lovebird suddenly appears on your computer monitor, keyboard, or ereader to figure out what you're looking at.

Lovebirds can't be happy left alone for long hours of the day. They crave to be part of a pair. A solo bird, kept apart from friends and family, can become so depressed it develops bad habits like tearing out its feathers or screaming a loud, persistent shrill cry for attention.

However, all is not lost if you really don't have time for an intense one-on-one relationship with a lovebird. Why not consider a pair? A pair of lovebirds can be beautiful, fun to watch, and surprisingly low maintenance, since they turn their focus toward each other instead of toward you.

Do you already have other pets?

WE'VE ALL SEEN THEM— those oh-so-cute Instagram photographs of a curious bird playing with somebody's cat or dog. Just... don't. The chance of disaster is huge. Lovebirds don't know their own size. They can't resist trying to intimidate much larger pets or even other humans. A bossy lovebird could dive-bomb your cat at exactly the wrong time to trigger an attack.

Some birds are happy as an only pet, and a hand-fed baby lovebird bonded to you ranks highly in that category. If your attention is already divided between other pets in the home, the time is probably not right to add a lovebird to the mix.

People sometimes joke around and say the bird should be called a hate-bird instead of a lovebird. Be aware that they are extremely strong and aggressive for their size. A lovebird can injure and kill other pet birds that it perceives as rivals. I have seen a lovebird dive-bomb a large Amazon parrot. They are completely fearless. Even though they are small, you should not add lovebirds to mixed-species aviaries of other birds. Somebody will get hurt.

Are you very sensitive to noise?

WHILE I WOULDN'T CONSIDER lovebirds the noisiest birds around, some of them— especially the peach-faced lovebird— have a shrill, piercing call that can really get on your nerves. You may want to listen to some of these birds on YouTube before you make a final decision about whether this species is right for you. Neglected lovebirds who can hear you moving elsewhere in the house can develop a truly obnoxious screaming habit, so be confident you'll have time for your pet before you bring it home.

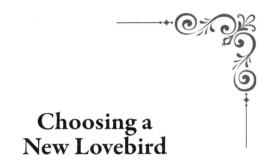

Choosing a New Lovebird

THE PEACH-FACED LOVEBIRD is one of the most available and easy-to-find pet birds in most areas, so you don't have to rush into making a decision. Masked and Fischer's lovebirds will be fairly easy to find as well. That said, you may still have to do a little searching around.

In many areas, it has become less common for pet stores or breeders to allow walk-in traffic. That isn't a bad thing. Closed aviaries can help protect the health of baby birds, and pet supply stores that don't sell birds can cut down on the number of impulse purchases.

There are plenty of lovebirds floating around, but responsible sellers are more cautious about screening buyers to make sure they know what they're getting into. Be patient with the process.

(Note: If you already know you're getting an older bird, you can skip ahead to the chapter on adopting older birds.)

Ask around. Network. There's nothing wrong with exploring dedicated Facebook groups and bird clubs, as long as you're good at rising above interpersonal drama. Some people are militantly anti-breeder, but I'm not a fan of those who want to pit breeders against rescues. There's a place for responsible breeders, and there's a place for rescue.

Lovebirds are small, but they are strong-willed. If you have never owned a bird before, a rescue lovebird may not be the right choice for you. You may do best if you bond early with a hand-fed baby. There is absolutely nothing wrong with that. You do your due diligence, and make the choice that's right for you and your bird.

Worth knowing: Juvenile lovebirds still have black markings on their beaks. An adult lovebird who has never been tamed can be very, very difficult to make into a pet. If you're paying for a hand-fed baby, double-check to be sure that's what you're getting.

Ask the seller about any health guarantees. Some breeders may offer you a short period of time to get your new bird checked out by an independent vet. Take advantage of that opportunity.

This author believes no beginner should ever buy sick or injured birds. Please make every effort to buy a strong, healthy bird from a responsible operation.

Everybody starts out planning to buy a healthy bird. However, the con artists in the community have developed every trick in the book for playing on the soft hearts of bird lovers. If you become aware of an abusive situation, report it to the local authorities. Don't try to fix it yourself by buying the birds. Don't give unethical people a financial incentive to remain in the bird breeding business.

You want to reward ethical breeders who truly care about their birds.

Make sure the breeder knows why you want the lovebird. If you want a pair to make a fine display in a small aviary, you will want two birds who get along with each other. If you want a single bird to be a pet, you want a hand-fed baby.

A lovebird who wasn't hand-fed can be a real handful. They want to bond with another lovebird, rather than with a mere human.

The lovebird destined to be a personal pet should be hand-fed from an early age, so they can imprint on a human as a potential friend and partner. You want your young lovebird to arrive in your home already knowing that humans are their friends. Some breeders may allow you to visit your baby during the weaning process. They may even sell you the bird or allow you to put a deposit on your baby.

However, a responsible breeder will never, ever send an inexperienced person home with an unweaned baby. You must be able to prove your ability and past experience to wean the bird.

Here again is an area where a con artist might play on your love for birds. The slob breeder who doesn't feel like going through the entire weaning process may weave a compelling story about how you, the newbie lovebird owner, can develop a richer bond by weaning the bird yourself. Actually, they just want to cut their hours and get to the money.

Hand-weaning a baby bird the size of a lovebird is a skill developed with lots of practice with the help of a more experienced hand-feeder. It isn't something you can do perfectly on your own at home in your spare time. Most people who pick up this book don't have the experience to hit all the marks you need to hit to safely wean a baby bird.

Check this step-by-step list of items you'd need to know:

*How to set-up a safe, sterile brooder.

*The exact temperature, humidity, and lighting combination needed to prevent the growth of bacteria while encouraging the growth of the young lovebird.

*How to prepare the formula at the exact temperature and consistency for each stage in the baby's development.

*How much your lovebird should weigh each day, and how to weigh your new baby.

*How to recognize signs the baby isn't developing normally.

*How to recognize signs the baby isn't properly digesting the formula.

There are multiple ways an inexperienced handfeeder can lose a young baby:

*Crop stasis. The food is not being digested or moving properly through the crop.

*Aspiration. Food going down the wrong pipe into the baby's lungs is often fatal to baby birds.

*Burning the crop.

*Feeding too much and causing the baby to regurgitate the food.

*Feeding too little or the wrong formula, causing the baby to suffer from malnutrition or dehydration.

If your breeder wants you to come in where they can provide expert, hands-on help in feeding the young lovebird, that's a great learning opportunity. But if the breeder is pushing you to take an unweaned baby home to feed without experienced supervision, that's a red flag.

Bird-Proof
Your Home

IF YOU'VE OWNED A PET bird before, you will probably be aware of most of this information. You can use this chapter as a quick checklist to make sure your home will be a safe, welcoming place for your new lovebird.

If you're a first-time bird owner, you will need to review this chapter with more care. Some hazards in our homes may surprise you, because it isn't obvious that something like a non-stick cooking pan or a potted avocado plant could kill a lovebird. Take the time to study this information and then to go through your home looking for potential problems before your new bird moves in.

Throw Out All Your Non-Stick PTFE Cookware

YOUR FIRST STOP IS the kitchen. Polytetrafluoroethylene (PTFE) is the chemical coating placed on non-stick cookware like Teflon to make it easier to clean. If you accidentally overheat or burn an item during cooking, this chemical releases an invisible toxin that overwhelms the sensitive lungs of birds. It works fast. Many victims have reported that every bird in an entire multi-room house or apartment has been killed within twenty minutes.

Some people have also reported mild flu-like symptoms as a result of PTFE poisoning, although humans can be expected to recover their health. Birds rarely survive.

Your lovebird has a life expectancy of over twenty years. It would be unrealistic to assume nobody in your household ever burns a pan in twenty years. I strongly recommend you to throw away all non-stick cookware coated with Teflon or any other coating that contains PTFE.

The time you save using a non-stick product is simply not worth the risk.

Consider Your Houseplants

LOVEBIRDS AREN'T THE chewiest parrots going, but they do explore and chew. Take a walk around the places where your new bird will spending time— the cage or aviary, the parrot playgym, the places you'll sit with your pet on your knee, arm, or shoulder. Consider each and every plant within the range of a curious beak.

Many popular houseplants are poisonous to pet birds. You will want to sell or give away these plants before your new pet comes home.

Low-light Lovers— It's a sad reality that many plants beloved for their ability to grow in dim corners and to thrive on neglect are poisonous. For example, *Dieffenbachia* contains needle-shaped crystals called raphides. Its nickname, Dumb Cane, comes from the fact that humans who chew on it sometimes lose their ability to speak, as well as experiencing a number of other unpleasant symptoms. Adults know better than to chew on the greenery, but both small children and pets have been poisoned by sampling the leaves.

Two other popular beauties, *Monstera* and *Philo-dendron,* are also widely regarded as hazardous to chewing pets.

*Avocado— Many people enjoy growing small potted trees from the pits of grocery store avocados. Unfortunately, avocado contains a natural fungicide which is deadly to parrots, including lovebirds. Give away your potted avocado to households without parrots.

*Holiday Plants— Poinsettia, holly, and mistletoe are all reported to be poisonous to pet birds. Since there are credible artificial options for the holiday season, consider giving away your living poinsettia, holly, and mistletoe to non-bird homes.

There are thousands of species of plants, and you may not be able to find out for sure if any given plant is safe. If you're not sure, make sure your bird is never given access to the plant in question.

Of course, there are many plants that are safe or even healthy for your lovebird.

Millet sprouts— Lovebirds are seed-eaters that often forage on the ground, and they have a special love for seeding grasses. The seeding heads of fresh-grown millet can be a special treat. The main problem with millet is that it can literally grow like a weed if it escapes into your lawn.

Spider Plant— This popular, hardy houseplant is beloved for its ability to create "babies" and keep growing larger and larger with a fairly minimal amount of care. As a bonus, the NASA Clean Air Study proved that they can help absorb common air pollutants found indoors like formaldehyde.

Boston Fern— Another hardy hanging basket favorite, this fern is another of the plants in the NASA Clean Air Study. They describe it as non-toxic but capable of absorbing formaldehyde out of polluted indoor environments.

Chia Pets— This fun-to-grow houseplant isn't a true cereal or grass. Instead, it's a member of the mint family. Either way, it's both edible and fun to grow. Some people even allow their small pet birds to sample their chia plants on purpose, because they are said to be rich in Omega-3 fatty acid, which is good for your bird's feathers.

Inspect the New Cage or Aviary

WE'LL TAKE A LONGER look at how to properly house your new lovebird in the next chapter. For now, it's important to know that you should already have a suitable cage or aviary ready for your new pet.

Are you building the cage yourself? In that case, you should check your materials and complete the construction thirty to ninety days in advance. All parrots, including lovebirds, are susceptible to a form of zinc poisoning called "new wire disease." A form of heavy metal poisoning, this disease occurs when a bird chews new galvanized wire or other new galvanized hardware like nuts and bolts.

New galvanized wire and hardware reacts to the environment by developing a powdery coat of zinc. Therefore, it needs to be weathered for up to three months before it will be safe for the birds to move in. You can speed up the process some by scrubbing down the galvanized hardware with white vinegar, but most people still say you should age this material at least thirty days.

The alternate option, of course, is to construct the new cage from a different material.

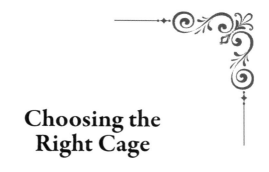

Choosing the Right Cage

THERE ARE MANY GOOD commercial cages on the market. Alas, there are also many bad ones. It's worth investing the time to make the right choice. A powder-coated metal cage can be an excellent option, as long as it's large enough. Unless it's only used as a sleep cage, you want to provide a minimum area of around eighteen inches wide by eighteen inches tall by twenty-two to twenty-four inches long.

Lovebirds are active birds who can get rough and rowdy with their toys, and you'll want to give them plenty of space to exercise their energy. A small cage won't save space the way you think it will, since any room where a lovebird comes out to play needs to be properly bird-proofed. Otherwise, you may be startled at how fast your favorite book or magazine is reduced to shreds.

Most commercial cages will include a removable metal grate. Peach-faced lovebirds in particular will enjoy making paper liners into confetti ribbons. If you want to discourage this practice, you can use the grate to make it more challenging for them to chew up the paper. If you don't mind supplying plenty of chewing paper, by all means, remove the grate and let them have at it.

Every good lovebird cage should be supplied with chewable perches and toys that you expect to replace on a regular basis. Never punish your lovebird for destroying a perch or a toy. Chewing is good exercise that helps the bird maintain the health of its beak. You may have one or two perches made of manzanita or another long-lasting material, but most of the available perches should be easy-to-chew wood like birch. Avoid perches with those sandpaper surfaces sold to trim the nails. They may or may not work, and they can irritate your pet's feet, causing red sores.

All toys should be rated for lovebirds or even stronger birds like small conures. Some small plastic items labeled as "bird toys" are only intended for budgerigars.

By the way, lovebirds really seem to enjoy taking out their aggressions on toy bells. Make sure the bell you provide is safe for a lovebird. Sometimes, they'll really play rough with their bell.

You will also need to buy or build a playgym. Many people start with a portable playgym that they can move from room to room, but they eventually graduate to leaving different gyms set up in all the places where the lovebird spends a lot of time.

Your lovebird's favorite playground can sometimes be your shoulder or the back of your neck, which means you should also keep on hand a supply of old shirts or smocks you can throw on when you're at home. I personally try to avoid allowing the bird to climb into pockets where they can be forgotten. However, many people do teach their hand-fed babies to become pocket pets.

Whatever you do, always be aware of where your lovebird is playing at any given time. Many lovebirds are injured or killed every year because they scramble into a back pocket or investigate a chair where their human doesn't notice until too late.

Lovebirds are active, curious, and drawn to poking their beaks into places where they shouldn't be. Make a strong habit of knowing where your pet is at all times whenever you have the bird out to play.

Some important items to consider for the cage and playpen:

Cuttlebones or Mineral Blocks— A classic source of calcium. Many lovebirds may ignore it for long periods of time, but make sure you have a clean mineral block available for when your bird feels the urge.

Mite protectors— In days gone by, these once-popular pet store items were sold as a cage hanger. You hung it on the cage, and somehow your lovebird would be magically protected from mites. They don't work, so you can take this item off the to-do list.

Millet Holder— Most lovebirds can't pick up and hold their own food in their foot. If you watch a small conure eat and then watch a lovebird eat, you will quickly see the difference. You can hold out the branch of millet for your bird yourself, but sometimes you need your hands free to do something else. That's where the millet holder comes in handy.

Lovebird Toys— Buy toys from reputable suppliers that are specifically designed for lovebirds. Your bird will be chewing and scrambling on these items, so you want them to be safe. Some people offer their lovebirds those little plastic mirrors. I do not. Lovebirds can be among those whose birds who believe a reflection in a mirror is a potential rival or lover. As a result, the mirror can spark aggressive or possessive behaviors, and most lovebirds are already aggressive enough as it is.

Travel Cage or Carrier— A small travel cage gives you a convenient way to transport your lovebird to the vet, bird sitter, or groomer, as well as an easy way to move your bird to a new home, to a vacation destination, or during an evacuation for a natural emergency like a hurricane.

A word of caution: Don't use the travel cage ONLY for visits to the vet or groomer. Put treats in there from time to time. Use it as another playpen. Otherwise, your lovebird will form a negative association with the travel cage and give you more of an argument when you bring it out.

Most new bird owners plan to spend most of their time with their pet lovebird indoors. However, here are some issues to consider if you're thinking about building a large aviary outdoors for a flock.

Protection from Predators Large and Small

ALL BIRDS ARE EDIBLE. A small parrot like a lovebird can attract a surprising number of potential enemies, including rodents, snakes, cats, raccoons, and even birds of prey like hawks or owls. The most deadly enemy of all is often the mosquito that carries diseases like avian pox or West Nile Virus.

A good aviary must offer protection from all of these predators, both large and small. You will want to use two layers of screen— an inner layer of strong hardware cloth capable of keeping out the bigger predator and an outer layer of pet-proof non-chewable mosquito netting.

Protection from the Elements

ONE OF THE GREAT ADVANTAGES of an outdoor aviary is that your birds can enjoy natural sunlight, which helps their bodies make vitamin D3. Without this vitamin, your lovebirds can't properly use calcium, the mineral which helps build strong bones and eggshells. In their wild environment, lovebirds would have access to all the natural sunlight they need, but they are often deprived of this invisible source of vitamins in our homes.

However, this isn't a license for you to expose your lovebirds to extremes of heat or direct sunlight. Your birds must always have access to shade and a place where they can cool off out of the sun.

Lovebirds are also fairly tolerant of cooler temperatures, as long as they have been properly acclimated. Make sure they have a dry, warm roost box, and a winter flight or cage where they can be protected from frost.

Protection from Losing Your Birds

LOVEBIRDS ARE NOT USUALLY considered expensive birds who would attract the attention of a thief, but you still need basic security to protect your flock against people who act on impulse.

*A good privacy fence may keep people from seeing or accessing the aviary.

*Good locks should be installed on the gate and the aviary.

*Webcams or baby monitors can be an inexpensive way to keep track of who is coming and going.

Walk-in aviaries should have a double door (air-lock-style) system. Both doors should never be open at the same time.

Bringing the New Baby Home

THE BIG DAY HAS FINALLY arrived. Your baby lovebird is weaned and ready to come home.

Have the cage, playpen, and other supplies ready and waiting so you can give your new pet a smooth introduction to its new home. Everybody will be excited, but make an effort not to overwhelm your new pet with too many people and too many noises all at once. Hand-fed baby lovebirds aren't afraid of their humans, but anybody can become overwhelmed in a new situation. Speak in calm, relaxed tones. Keep the ambient noise low by playing soft music rather than loud games or violent television programs.

As a general rule, hand-fed lovebirds love being the center of attention, as long as you're not too pushy about it. (An exception: Some lovebirds have a phobia of human hands. We'll talk more about that in the chapter about behavior problems.) If you have other pets in the home, you will likely want to keep them well away from your new lovebird until you have a better handle on how well your baby behaves when it's out of the cage or carrier.

You should also supervise carefully to make sure children and other family members never grab the bird around its body. They may associate the feeling of being grabbed with the sensation of being captured by a predator. One careless grab could spark an enduring phobia.

Your breeder has probably already demonstrated the, "Step up" command to you. Some lovebirds learn to step on a perch that is inserted into their cage or brooder. Others step on a balled-up fist or your arm.

My personal preference is to never stick a hand into a parrot cage. Instead, I insert a perch and hold it against the bird's chest while saying, "Step up." Your new pet can then ride the perch until out in the open, where I can then offer the hand, arm, shoulder, or playpen.

Another good way to carry lovebirds is to shape your hand into an open cup. It probably isn't the hand itself they fear, so much as the sensation of being grabbed.

Some lovebirds are very fussy about exactly how they like to be carried. They may even have a special stick or perch they prefer. Experiment, but be relaxed about it. Your new baby could live fifteen to twenty years. There's no need to rush the process of discovery.

Lovebirds, like all parrots— even much larger ones— have a short attention span. Don't plan on a two-hour bonding session. Instead, plan multiple five to twenty-minute bonding sessions over the course of a day. Several short, enjoyable encounters are much better than a single long, tiring session. Since hand-fed babies don't fear humans, a grumpy baby can nip or bite. You always want to end the session on a positive note before it ever gets to that point.

Bringing Home
the Rescue or
Older Lovebird

OLDER LOVEBIRDS CAN present some real challenges, but they can also present different rewards.
There's no reason to reject an older bird out of hand, as
long as you properly prepare for your new pet's arrival.
Here are some common situations that crop up.

*You want to make a difference to a bird who
turned up in a rescue.

*You've been asked to take care of the lovebird after
the original owner went through some life changes that
made it impossible for them to keep their pet. If you al-

ready know the original owner, take advantage of the opportunity to learn as much as you can about the bird's history and its particular health and personality challenges. For instance, I was asked to rescue a pair of Fischer's lovebirds who were reported to be too noisy at dawn for their owner's small apartment where their cage was placed in an east-facing window. I set them up in a larger flight with a nest box that allowed them to sleep in longer without being disturbed by early morning light. The pair immediately ceased making the obnoxious morning calls.

*You have found a lost lovebird. Because their small size makes vets reluctant to microchip them, and because they can go quite a long distance from feeder to feeder, you may not be able to locate the original owner.

Any of these reasons are perfectly fine reasons to open your home to an older lovebird.

Never adopt an untamed wild adult thinking you will be able to transform the lovebird into a shoulder pet. Lovebirds are one genus of parrots that do need to be trained and tamed when they are still young. If the bird is wild and unsocialized, you will both probably be happier if you can find a second lovebird to be its companion.

Getting Off On the Right Foot

START BY GETTING A health exam, especially if you have other birds in the home. Protecting the pets you already have should always be your priority.

In an ideal world, you would always bring home your new lovebird during a relatively calm, stress-free period of your life when you can devote plenty of time and attention to your new bird. Life doesn't always work out that way. A sudden death or a disaster like a fire could leave you with a homeless bird who needs help today, whether or not your own situation is entirely ideal.

At the very least, be aware that a lovebird's big issue is being isolated. Keep your new pet with you as much as you can, even if you can't take it out of the carrier.

Seeing you and talking to you means a lot to a lovebird, especially one that was originally hand-fed by humans.

When you rescue a lovebird with an unknown history, you have to be somewhat sensitive. If your bird is very wild and doesn't know basic tricks like how to step up, you may have an aviary bird that can never be tamed. However, don't rush to judgment.

For instance, someone brought me a lost lovebird they found on the street that they described as, "vicious," and a "biter." I assumed the bird was lost from a breeder's aviary.

Not the case. Actually, the bird wasn't wild or vicious, and she has never bitten anyone in the years since her rescue.

When the bird was transferred to me, I got her alone in a quiet room and let her check me out before I offered her the chance to leave her carrier by stepping on a perch. It became obvious within minutes that she knew how to step on and off a stick, an arm, and a shoulder. She wasn't a lost aviary bird. She was somebody's lost pet.

So why did she make such a bad impression on the man who rescued her?

Because he started out by making a bad impression on *her*.

When he originally found the bird, he tried to pick her up in his hands, triggering her phobia. It would have been easy to make a mistake and assume she couldn't be tamed. Yet, all she really needed was a light touch and some patience.

What if you do discover that you have an older bird who has never been handled by humans or taught to step up? After all, lovebirds kept as part of a breeding pair or colony aren't particularly rare. In that case, you need to be realistic. Adult lovebirds who are imprinted on each other are very, very difficult to transform into affectionate pets.

Your best bet is probably to adopt a pair or colony of lovebirds together, so that your birds can socialize with each other. In that situation, you will be their chief cook and bottle-washer, rather than the center of their emotional life, but they can still fill your home with life and color.

Should You Trim Your Lovebird's Wings?

I USUALLY RECOMMEND that pet bird owners keep their lovebird's wings trimmed, even if they don't trim the wings of any other bird in their home. There are a couple of reasons for this.

*You are more likely to lose a flighted pet. Many people lose their lovebirds out a carelessly opened door or window every year. These little birds are curious and quick to take advantage of an opportunity to explore, but they are likely to become confused once they're out in the wider world. They don't know what your house looks like from the outside, and they may not be able to find their way home again.

I have rescued lovebirds who were clearly looking for someone to take care of them, probably their previous owner. However, because of the distance they had wandered, I wasn't able to find their original owners and ended up placing them in new homes.

Most populated areas of the world present significant hazards to an escaped seed-eating bird that likes to feed on the ground where seeding grasses grow. Cats, dogs, rats, snakes, hawks, owls, and even blue jays and mockingbirds can present a problem. At least one peach-faced lovebird has been photographed scrapping with a mockingbird shortly before its rescue.

*Flighted lovebirds can become aggressive. Hand-fed lovebirds can be sweet as pie when they want to be, but they can also appoint themselves to be tiny terrors. Hand-fed peach-faced lovebirds, in particular, literally do not know their own size. This author finds it funny when a tiny lovebird whaps me on the head with its wings, but it really isn't a good idea to encourage this behavior. For the most part, a neatly trimmed lovebird is a lovebird with much better manners.

*Indoor lovebirds are less likely to run into walls, mirrors, or windows at dangerous speeds if they are clipped. A startled bird could take off faster than it means to. Running into a mirror or a window at full speed can stun a lovebird or even result in a broken neck.

As grass-eating parrots, they are evolved to enjoy walking and climbing around, so lovebirds have other ways to exercise. In fact, clipping the wings may give them more opportunities to be out for exercise, since you are more likely to take them out on their parrot play gym when you don't have to worry about aggressive behaviors or accidental injuries.

Important to know: A wing clip is not permanent surgery. You are not really clipping the wings. You are clipping the fully grown-out primary feathers. You never cut into living, growing blood feathers. Therefore, a properly performed clip doesn't hurt the bird any more than a properly performed haircut hurts you.

However, just as hair grows back, feathers grow back too. Keep an eye on the molt. Sooner or later, you will need to return to the groomer for another trim, or else your lovebird will be fully flighted once again. I soon notice the change in attitude if I neglect to keep a lovebird's feathers properly trimmed.

If you decide to keep a flighted lovebird

IF YOU DO DECIDE TO allow your lovebird's wings to grow out, you face some special challenges. You will need to take exceptional care to make sure your bird doesn't get lost in the wild. Develop strong habits. When you're home and have your bird out, make sure the doors and windows are secured from the inside. If someone opens a door to the outside unexpectedly, your curious pet could be halfway across town before you know it.

Some lovebirds love to cuddle up and go to sleep on your neck or shoulder. When they're snoozing quietly away, it's oh-so-easy to forget they're even there. If you walk outside with a bird on your shoulder, one bark from a neighbor's dog could startle your pet and send it flying away.

Make a habit of checking your shoulder and your bird's cage every time before you open the door to the outside world. Every. Single. Time.

There is such a thing as a lovebird flight harness, developed to allow people to fly their bird outside without being at risk for losing their pet. If you have a hand-fed baby who was handled from an early age, and you have continued to handle the bird with confidence, you may be able to slowly introduce your pet to the idea of the harness.

Leave it out for a few days near the cage or play-gym, so the bird can see the harness is completely harmless. Eventually, you can move forward with trying to put it on the bird.

Birds who are fearful of being grabbed or toweled are not likely to ever accept the harness. If you have the rare lovebird who enjoys being handled, you have the greatest chance of success.

Most people, though, will have the strongest bond with their pet lovebird if they keep the wings neatly and regularly trimmed.

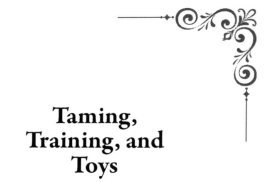

Taming, Training, and Toys

TAMING AND TRAINING a lovebird can be very, very easy, or it can be very, very hard, but it always— yes, always!— demands a significant investment in time. This author may be judged guilty of repeating herself, but I will say it once more for the people in the back:

Lovebirds demand time. They will *always* demand time.

If you ever get too busy to devote time to your single pet lovebird, you will need to find it a good companion. Neglected lovebirds shriek, tear out their own feathers, become overly aggressive, and eventually lose their tameness. All parrots are social, but these little birds are particularly dependent on having a partner that is physically as well as emotionally close to them.

It isn't enough to *feel* love for your lovebird. You must *demonstrate* that love by making your new pet an important part of your life.

This is not to guilt you if something happens, and life changes. If something happens that interferes with your ability to spend quality *and* quantity time with your lovebird, you have options like introducing your bird to a second bird who can be a fulltime companion. However, you had big dreams when you first adopted your lovebird— dreams of a special pet who trusted and relied on you. Those dreams will only be fulfilled if you have the time to fulfill them.

Don't adopt a lovebird if your life is going crazy. Adopt a lovebird at a time when you've got time.

Enough. This author has said it before, and she'll say it again. You get it.

Even the sweetest, most accepting hand-fed baby lovebird needs your time and presence.

So. Moving on. For some, your brand new baby lovebird will seem like a deceptively easy pocket pet. The bird comes already tame, thanks to the work of the hand-feeder. The bird already wants to bond with somebody, thanks to its own instinct to form a tight pair bond. Everything is already in place. All you have to do is show up and let the magic happen.

Well. Yes and no.

There is no shortcut to forming a good bond. You have to spend a lot of time, every day, with your pet. Lovebirds are capable of losing their tameness if you don't. And it can be very tough to get that tameness back.

This is a major reason why individual pet lovebirds sometimes seem to do better with people who are retired or who work out of home offices. The hand-fed baby lovebird came to them already tame, and they have the time to invest in *keeping* the bird tame.

A pair or colony can remain in their aviary, but a single lovebird needs time out of its cage. As we mentioned earlier, you can set up a play area in each room where you spend a lot of time with the bird, or you can use a portable play gym. You should also devote time each day to allowing your bird to play on your arm or shoulder. Non-phobic lovebirds should also be asked to step on and off your fist or hand, the better to keep them from developing a phobia toward human hands.

All solo pet parrots should be taught the Step Up command. A pet lovebird that steps onto a hand, arm, fist, or perch on command will be infinitely easier to move around with you in the course of a day. For example, say your lovebird has flown to a high perch. You can offer the stick while saying, "Step up," and a well-trained bird will climb onto the stick. Life is easier when you can fetch a bird from a high perch and move it back onto a play gym or into a sleep cage without a lot of negotiation.

If you're starting with a hand-fed, domestic-bred lovebird, you shouldn't have much trouble teaching this basic command. In some cases, the seller may have already taught the bird this command. If not, you start by getting your new bird used to being around you. Make sure the bird knows that you are now the person who is offering the food and treats like millet.

Then you build on a parrot's natural instinct to always move to the highest available perch. Hold the perch at your lovebird's chest level and offer the treat in your other hand, a little above the perch so that the bird has to step up to get the treat. Your pet will soon figure it out.

You also need to practice moving your bird from perch to perch. A tightly bonded lovebird could be difficult to peel off your shirt if it hasn't learned to step off your arm on command. But it's a pretty easy variation on what your bird already knows how to do. Say your bird is already on your arm, and you'd like to bird to step onto an empty perch on the playgym or in the cage.

Simply move the perched bird so the empty perch is at breast level. Now, when you give the command to, "Step On," the bird will be moving to the new perch.

This author likes to practice these commands with a sort of ladder game. Hold the perch at your bird's breast level, and say, "Step On." Then offer a new perch at breast level. And so on. Don't be annoying. Do it a few times a few minutes at a time. The lessons should be fun.

Caution: Older lovebirds are resistant to change, and sometimes can't really be tamed, only trained to perform a trick in response to a clicker. Good animal trainers can train adult lovebirds— after all, they can even train lions and tigers— but an amateur is unlikely to enjoy much success without a great deal of time and patience to invest in the training.

What About Talking?

LOVEBIRDS ARE PARROTS. This author has heard it said that every species of parrot includes at least a few individuals who can talk. Yes, there are even those rare few lovebirds who can talk. However, the odds that you'll be able to teach your lovebird to talk are remote.

And, even if you do, peach-faced lovebirds in particular tend to have rather high, shrill voices that are not terribly easy to understand.

If you want to try, here are some tips:

*Pick a phrase instead of a one-syllable word. When the voice is unclear, the brain more easily understands a short phrase like, "Pretty bird," as opposed to a single word like, "Hi." Your friends may perceive the single word as just another tweet.

*A phrase repeated in a higher pitch is more likely to catch your bird's attention than a phrase repeated in a lower pitch. Small children's voices are shrill and attention-getting but unclear. Therefore, a higher-pitched adult woman's voice is usually best for the job of teaching lovebirds or any other parrot.

*Consider recording the phrase and allowing it to play while you're not present.

*Birds, like people, tune out any sound that is repeated endlessly. The best lessons allow the bird to hear the phrase for a short period of time, such as five minutes, then rests the sound, then lets it play again for another five minutes. Several short sessions during the day are much more likely to inspire your lovebird to copy the sound than one hour-long session.

*Most lovebirds never learn to say a single human word. Our pets should be accepted for who they are, not for who we wish they were. Remember, there are many enjoyable ways to engage with our pets. Most lovebirds will enjoy batting a bell around while swearing in their own language much more than they will enjoy trying to pick up our languages. If the lessons stop being fun, feel free to abandon the lessons.

What To Feed A Lovebird

IN A SENSE, LOVEBIRDS are easy to feed because they evolved to eat seed, which is easy to find, buy, store, and serve. However, a wild lovebird undoubtedly forages far and wide over the course of a lifetime, eating not just dry seed but fresh seeding grasses, sprouts, and perhaps even a protein-rich insect or two. Lovebirds might not need as extensive and expensive a diet as many parrots, but they won't live up to their potential if they are kept strictly on a diet of dry seed and water.

Every year, many lovebirds kept only on seeds die far too young from diet-related diseases like egg binding, liver disease, and vitamin deficiencies.

You want to offer a seed-based, **not** a seed-only diet. Make sure the mix is a high-quality seed formula designed specifically for lovebirds, who prefer smaller seeds like millet and canary seed in addition to oilseeds like sunflower and safflower. You should also offer access to finely chopped vegetables that includes such items as turnip tops, collard greens, mustard greens, kale, Swiss chard, dandelion greens, chickweed, fresh or frozen sweet corn, grated carrot, grated zucchini, broccoli florets, snow peas, spinach, and bell pepper. Clean, fungus-free sprouts, including sprouting millet, is often a well-accepted treat.

It can be a struggle to get a lovebird to recognize chopped salad as food. As a result, many people have developed various birdie bread recipes to tempt their pets into eating a more varied diet. You can bake a loaf if you have several birds, but if you have only one or two lovebirds, you should probably make muffins. In that way, you can freeze some of the muffins for a future date.

There are many recipes available online. Many were developed for cockatiels, who are also stubborn and picky seed eaters, but they can be used to tempt lovebirds just as well.

Here is one recipe to get you started.

Sweet Potato Cockatiel Bread

SWEET POTATO, YAM, grated carrot, or pumpkin are all valuable vegetables for helping both cockatiels and lovebirds consume enough beta carotene, which converts to vitamin A in a bird's body. Although sweet potato recipes are widely available for humans, you need to cut way back on the sugar and spices when adapting them for pet birds.

The powdered eggshell, which makes this recipe a bit too crunchy for human tastes, is a valuable source of calcium.

Ingredients

1-3/4 cup all-purpose flour

1 tablespoon baking powder

1 tablespoon brown sugar

½ cup finely chopped walnuts

½ cup finely chopped raisins, dried cranberries, dates, or figs

2 large clean eggs including the shell

¾ cup unsweetened apple juice

1 cup cooked mashed yams, sweet potatoes, carrots, or pumpkin

¼ cup canola oil

Preheat the oven to 425 degrees Fahrenheit. Grease the muffin tin or loaf pan. Stir together the dry ingredients. Crack the eggs, and carefully crush the shells as fine as you can with a wooden cooking mallet. Add the powdered shell to the other dry ingredients. Scramble the eggs with a fork, and then mix together with the apple juice, mashed vegetable, and oil. Blend into the dry ingredients.

You can now spoon the bread batter into the loaf or muffin pan. Cooking time depends on your oven, as well as the size of your muffins or loaves, but I set the timer for 25 minutes and keep checking every five or ten minutes after that. The bread is done when you can stick a knife in the center, and it comes away clean, without any sticky batter on it.

Let cool, then remove the bread from the pan. Individual muffins can be kept in the freezer for a couple of weeks and defrosted the same day you want to serve them to your birds.

Some people who offer a seed-based diet may choose to supply a good lovebird pellet as ten percent of the diet instead of offering the birdie bread. A lot depends on how much time you like to devote to food preparation, as well as to close observation of what foods your bird actually eats.

An Alternative Diet

SOME LOVEBIRD OWNERS, especially in North America, are fans of the modern pelleted diet. A stubborn lovebird who picks out only its favorite seeds can be at risk of a nutritional deficiency. Avian vets and nutritionists have worked to develop a pellet which supplies balanced nutrition in every bite.

If your hand-fed baby lovebird was brought up on pellets, you have a fairly easy job. Simply continue to offer the recommended pellets as the core of the diet. Chopped vegetables, birdie bread, soft cooked corn, and millet sprays can be offered on the side as a special treat.

Alas, if your lovebird was raised on seed, you are in for a real battle if you try to switch to pellets. These birds are strong-willed, and their opinions aren't usually subject to change once they're mature. You can try to make the switch, but many lovebirds will never accept the pellets if they weren't brought up on them from the beginning.

If you do decide to make the switch, buy a small kitchen gram scale, and make a note of your bird's weight each day. This is not a weight-loss diet. A starving bird is not healthier than a bird who eats nothing but seed. Even with the advice of your avian vet or a more experienced lovebird owner, you may find that converting to pellets is a long, drawn-out process. It isn't something this author recommends you to try on a whim.

You have not failed as a pet owner if your lovebird refuses to eat pellets. Keep in mind that many popular parrots like conures are from moist, rich, tropical climates where they would eat a variety of fruits and vegetables, not just seeding grasses. Cockatiels, budgerigars, and lovebirds come from a climate that is dryer and much less lush. They can be more conservative and less adventurous when it comes to their food, and that's perfectly natural.

Supplements

AS A GENERAL RULE, lovebirds who eat a pellet-based diet get enough vitamins and minerals from the pellets. Those lovebirds who prefer a seed-based diet should have a good avian vitamin and mineral supplement powder that can be sprinkled on soft food they're willing to eat, such as berries or greens. There are medical situations that may require you to offer special supplements such as calcium, but you should give these supplements on the advice of a vet who has examined your bird.

What Not to Feed a Lovebird

THERE'S ONE POSITIVE aspect to the lovebird's lack of an adventurous palate. Some parrots want to taste everything you eat, but you should have less trouble keeping problem foods out of your lovebird's beak. For the record, here are some items to avoid.

*Avocado and guacamole. As we mentioned in the section on houseplants, avocado contains a natural fungicide called persin. The fungicide is most concentrated in the pit, leaves, bark, and skin, but it may also appear in the edible fruit. Since persin is poisonous to parrots as well as to fungus, you should never share this food with your lovebird or include it in the birdie chopped salad.

*Caffeine and theobromine.** Both of these stimulants can be hazardous to a bird's heart. Caffeine is found in coffee, green and black teas, and some colas. Theobromine is found in chocolate. Both chemicals are stimulating to us, but could be harmful to your lovebird's heart.

*Alcohol.**

*Uncooked meat, fish, seafood, or poultry.**

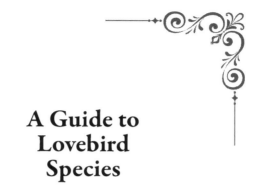

A Guide to Lovebird Species

ALL TRUE LOVEBIRDS are members of the genus *Agapornis*, which is found only on the continent of Africa and the large off-shore island of Madagascar.

Captive breeders and pet owners tend to classify the lovebirds in broad groups.

*White eye-ringed lovebird species that breed in colonies— masked, Fischer's, Lilian's, and black-cheeked lovebirds.

*Peach-faced— the best-known species which lacks an eye-ring but also breeds in colonies.

*Sexually dimorphic species— Madagascar, Abyssinian, and red-headed lovebirds. They can be sexed at a glance since males and females look different. However, each pair needs its own cage or flight for breeding, and they tend to be rare because they represent significant challenges to the breeder.

*Black-collared— The black-collared or Swindern's lovebird (*Agapornis swindernianus*) is rarely if ever kept in captivity. Unlike the more popular lovebirds, it makes an undesirable pet because it demands a rare African fig in its daily diet. Since you're unlikely to ever see it, we won't talk more about it.

While we're at it, we'll make quick work of the other three species you're unlikely to encounter as a new or intermediate lovebird hobbyist.

The grey-headed or Madagascar lovebird (*Agapornus canus*) is not difficult to spot in the wild, but they are said to become shy in captivity. The adults are easily sexed, since only the males have the gray heads and breasts, while the females are attractive shades of green all over. Since they are shy and don't show or breed well in captivity, they are considered a poor choice for a pet for any but the experienced breeder.

The black-winged or Abyssinian lovebird (*Agapornis taranta*) is the largest lovebird. Native to Eritrea and Ethiopia (the former Abyssinia), the adult males stand out because of their bold red foreheads, while the females have all-green heads. Their natural habitat is at fairly high elevations, and they are known to be hardly birds tolerant of cooler temperatures who can breed in nest boxes. However, they haven't caught on like the colony-nesting lovebirds and are rarely, if ever, encountered as pets.

The red-headed or red-faced lovebird (*Agapornis pullarius*) is a wide-ranging wild species destined to remain rare in aviculture because of its unusual nesting habits. The female tunnels out her own nest in a tree or ground termite mound. A few hard-working breeders have coaxed pairs into nesting in cork-lined nest boxes or human-constructed burrows, but the red-faced lovebird remains much more common in the wild than in captivity. Unlike the other two dimorphic species, the female is allowed a soft pop of orange color on her face. However, the male's brighter, deeper, and more extensive red-orange on both face and bill makes him easy to identify.

The Popular Pet Lovebirds and their Lookalikes

THE PEACH-FACED OR rosy-faced lovebird (*Agapornis roseicollis*) is the iconic lovebird. In the wild, they are small, short-tailed green parrots with peach-colored faces and throats, blue rumps, and a hint of mischief in their deep black eyes. There is no eye-ring. The sexes look alike.

They are widespread birds who feed on grass and seeds, allowing them to live in a variety of dry, scrubby, and even cultivated habitats. They are bold, gregarious, even pushy birds who breed in small colonies.

The females are famous for their habit of collecting scraps of nesting material and tucking it into their rumps like ribbons or streamers to be carried to the nest. In the wild, this material might be strips of bark or palm fronds. In captivity, they have an astounding ability to reduce magazines, books, calendars, and other paper items to confetti.

As you will see later, there are a great many color mutations in captivity. However, you can always recognize the peach-faced lovebird in any of its guises because of its lack of the eye-ring.

The four eye-ring species may present more of a challenge, especially to the new hobbyist. These four species— masked, Fischer's, Lilian's, and black-cheeked— are colony breeders, and they will hybridize with each other at will if you happen to mix them together. This is a very bad idea because hybridized birds can threaten the survival of the less common species, Lilian's and black-cheeked. If you're buying a single hand-fed baby as a pet, it probably doesn't much matter to you whether the bird is a masked, a Fischer's, a hybrid, or whoever. The care will be much the same.

However, if you are buying a pair, and you intend to breed your bird, it does matter. Be sure to get your birds from a well-regarded breeder who can give you the background on your lovebirds.

The masked or yellow-collared lovebird (*Agapornis personatus*) is probably the second most popular species of lovebird, right after the peach-faced. In the wild form, they are striking birds with their bright white eye-ring around a black eye on a black head. The bill is lipstick red, and there is a yellow collar or yoke around the neck and breast.

The blue color mutations are just as striking. The bright white eye-ring now matches with a bright white yoke, while the green parts on the wild bird are replaced with shades of blue.

The first blue color mutation was actually found in wild birds almost a century ago, but today breeders have developed a large variety of color mutations.

Fischer's lovebirds (*Agapornis fischeri*) are an exceptionally beautiful species in the wild. Like masked lovebirds (a close relative), they have a yellow breast but it shades up into an orange rather than a black face. You might ask how anyone could improve on perfection, but several mutations, including some beautiful blues, are widely available.

A close relative and lookalike of Fischer's is the Lilian's or Nyasa lovebird (*Agapornis lilianae*), a near-threatened species which is vanishing in the wild. Unfortunately, it could also be endangered in captivity because of many, many years of hybridization with the Fischer's lovebird. A true Lilian's is a tiny lovebird with a green rump. A Lilian's with some blue feathers in the rump may be a hybrid that should be kept only as a pet or aviary bird, rather than a breeder.

The black-cheeked lovebird (*Agapornis nigrigenis*), which looks something like a smaller masked lovebird that lacks the yellow collar, is another species threatened in aviculture because of frequent interbreeding with its bigger cousin. This vulnerable upland species is native to Zambia, where its population continues to fall because of habitat destruction and collection for the pet trade.

The care of all four eye-ring species and their hybrids is similar, especially if you are keeping a single pet.

However, if you ever plan to breed your lovebird, you want to know exactly what you have so you can make a suitable match that improves, rather than harms, the future of the species.

A Few Words About Lovebird Mutations

BREEDING AND SHOWING lovebirds can become an addictive hobby for a variety of reasons.

*The challenge of being the first to develop a new mutation.

*The excitement of opening a new nest full of healthy babies.

*The thrill of winning a prize for best in show.

The great variety of color mutations available is one of the key reasons that people around the world have fallen in love with lovebirds. Be aware that entire books have been written on lovebird mutations. Consider this chapter an introduction, not the final word, on the subject.

In fact, if you're keeping a solo pet, you can probably skim this section or even skip it altogether if you want to.

However, if you're curious about color mutations, stick around. To make sure we're all on the same page, let's review some basic information.

A **genus** is made up of a group of closely related species found in the wild. All true African lovebirds are members of the genus *Agapornis*. With birds, members of a genus tend to be such close relatives that they can all breed with each other if placed together by accident or on purpose. As we mentioned earlier, this is definitely the case with *Agapornis*. To preserve the individual species in captivity, you need to take care that you never, ever hybridize your lovebirds.

There are nine **species** of *Agapornis* lovebirds, eight found on the African continent and one found offshore on the large island of Madagascar. For example, peach-faced lovebird is the name of the entire species. It is fine to breed different color mutations within a single species. What isn't fine it to breed two members from different species.

To reiterate:

Hybridizing lovebirds can put the rarer species at risk of extinction both in captivity and in the wild. Always breed peach-faced lovebirds with other peach-faced lovebirds, Fischer's lovebirds with other Fischer's lovebirds, and so on.

Of course, the popular lovebirds that are bred in captivity can appear in many different color **mutations**. Again, a mutation is not a different species, just a different look. For example, a Sea Green mutation of the peach-faced lovebird is still a peach-faced lovebird.

You knew all that, but we're making it crystal clear before we move on to the tough stuff.

The African Love Bird Society has posted this statement:

"Most major bird organizations frown on hybridization. ALBS has always been opposed to hy-

bridization and does not allow the exhibition of obviously hybridized birds. If you want to allow your birds to breed, please find appropriate partners for them that are of the same species."

This policy isn't there to spoil anybody's fun. It's there to protect the future of the five (or more) species bred in captivity. You can breed any color pairs you like within the species, but do make sure all pairs are matched with members of their own species.

As you consider the large number of lovebird mutations available, you'll hear three terms over and over again that you'll want to know. Again, this is a quick overview, not a doctorate-level course in avian genetics, so take these simplified definitions as a starting point. If you decide to get serious about breeding mutations, you will need much more than this little book.

(And you can feel free to skip over the next few paragraphs if this is too technical for you. Not everyone will want or need this information.)

*Dominant— A dominant trait will be expressed. You don't have to wonder if the bird is carrying a hidden gene for the trait. For example, with peach-faced lovebirds, the Normal or Green colors found in the wild are dominant.

It's an over-simplification for all genes, but for color mutation genes, you can usually assume that a bird gets one gene from each parent for any given trait. If the bird gets a dominant trait from one parent and a recessive trait from the other, the dominant trait is the one that will be expressed.

*Recessive— A recessive trait can therefore be hidden. It will only be expressed if the bird gets a copy of the gene for the recessive trait from *both* parents. For example, in peach-faced lovebirds, the color blue is recessive. In the wild, this gene is rare, and the odds of a baby inheriting it from both parents is very low, so wild blue peach-faced lovebirds are rarely if ever seen.

In captivity, the trait is more common, because humans like the color blue, and breeders have worked to create many blue lovebird mutations.

Many captive-bred lovebirds carry both a dominant and a hidden (recessive) trait. Birds like this are called splits, because their genes are split between the dominant and the recessive one.

If you happen to breed two splits who have the same hidden trait, and they both pass the hidden trait to one of their youngsters, you can have a baby who grows up looking very different from either one of the parents.

*Sex-Linked— These traits are a little more tricky for most of us to understand. With sex-linked recessive traits, the female gets only one gene. The female gets the gene, and she expresses it. She can't be split to a sex-linked trait because the gene can't be masked by a more dominant trait.

However, the male receives a gene from each parent as usual. The dominant gene will express itself if it's there. Therefore, he can be "split" with a hidden recessive gene in his DNA.

You might be wondering if that's right. Yes, avian genetics is a little bit like Opposites Day compared to human genetics. Human males have only one X chromosome. In birds, males are the ones who have two X chromosomes, while females have only one. So, if all of this sounds backward to you, now you know why.

Many popular mutations are sex-linked, including the Cinnamon and the Pearl.

Why is this important?

Females get only one gene for any given sex-linked mutation, a gene donated by their father. However, the males get a gene from each parent. He would need to get the same sex-linked recessive gene from both of his parents to express that gene. Therefore, it's possible for a male bird to carry a hidden gene for a sex-linked trait that he can pass down to his own youngsters even though he doesn't express the trait himself.

You can make predictions about a pair's offspring based on what mutations the parents express.

For example, consider the ever-popular Lutino mutation in peach-faced lovebirds. The green trait has been bred out of these birds, which leaves a lovely yellow individual with a bright peachy-red face and forehead. Breeders know from experience that the Lutino mutation is sex-linked in this lovebird species.

This means, if both parents are Lutino, all of the offspring will also turn out to be Lutino.

However, if the male is a Lutino, and the female is a Normal Green, the male offspring will all look like Normal Greens but will carry a hidden gene for the Lutino mutation. By contrast, all female offspring will be Lutino. This means you can visually sex your baby birds from that pair from the time their feathers begin to appear.

If the female parent is the Lutino, and the male is the Normal Green, all of your babies will look like Normal Greens. None of the female offspring will carry the Lutino gene. However, the trait is not lost. All of the males will be split for the Lutino gene and thus have the potential to pass it on to a future generation.

If you're confused, relax. There is no reason to get lost in the weeds all by yourself. As we already mentioned, lovebird genetics is an absorbing and rewarding hobby that supports serious breeders and exhibitors. You can join breeder's and exhibitor's organizations to learn from experts who can lead you deeper into this fascinating world. For example, the African Love Bird Society (ALBS) is an international society devoted to the care, breeding, and exhibiting of all species in the *Agapornis* genus. Another good group is Agapornis Breeders & Exhibitors International, which has hosted online an extensive collection of photographs and information about the various mutations.

For now, we'll touch very briefly on some of the possibilities.

Peach-faced Lovebirds

THE NORMAL, WILD, OR Green peach-faced lovebird is an exceptionally attractive bird with a variety of pigments in its plumage, including greens, blues, roses, and reds. This large palette of color allows breeders to employ selective breeding techniques to create birds in an astonishing variety of color and patterns. When you keep in mind that color mutations can be combined, you begin to understand why one source claims there are over one hundred thousand color varieties of this species in captivity around the world.

Needless to say, it gets complicated. But it all starts with the base color. Peach-faced lovebirds belong to one of two broad color series.

*Green. The green, normal, wild, or wild green trait is the dominant one, which is why it's the one found in almost one hundred percent of wild birds. Just to make things confusing, the face is not actually peach-colored. It's a bright rosy-red.

*Blue. The blue traits are recessive. There are variants of the blue series such as Dutch Blue or Aqua, White-faced Blue or Turquoise, and Sea Green or Aqua Turquoise. The face is usually a cream or white color, with a small peach marking on the forehead.

Of course, all shades of green or blue are not the same. With partial dominant or co-dominant traits, the young bird will show the trait even if only one parent passes on the gene. However, if both parents do happen to pass on the trait, the color mutation will be a deeper so-called Double Factor mutation. For example, jade and olive are shades of green that can appear as single or double factors.

Eye-ring Lovebird Mutations

MASKED LOVEBIRDS COME in almost as many mutations as the peach-faced itself, or so it seems. The blue masked lovebird is one of the more eye-catching lovebirds out there, thanks to its bright white eye-ring on a black face, which contrasts well with the white breast and blue wings and body. However, as with peach-faced lovebird, there are a large number of other mutations in a variety of patterns and color.

The Fischer's lovebird is a third species that comes in a wide variety of color mutations. A surprising number of these mutations result in the white eye-ring appearing on a white face, which makes it more difficult for the newbie to immediately recognize the bird as an eye-ring lovebird species.

Worth noting: In the eye-ring lovebird species, the Lutino mutation is NOT sex-linked the way it is in the peach-faced lovebird species. That means you can't use the appearance of the babies to figure out their gender.

Common Lovebird Behavior Problems

LOVEBIRDS CAN BE A strong-willed species. If you have ever heard the phrase, "small dog syndrome," you understand the concept. A hand-fed lovebird has no idea of its own size, and a badly socialized pet can become a holy terror. Small parrots aren't always guaranteed to stay well-socialized. You must have time and affection to lavish on them. Their pair-bond is strong. A lonely, isolated lovebird can dream up a lot of ways to make your life a living misery.

You must work within your lovebird's natural psychology. They can never understand being kept alone for long hours at a time. If your bird feels neglected, you can face a whole range of problems including screaming, biting, and plucking.

Let's take a look at some common problems, and what you can do to prevent or fix them.

My bird is afraid of hands.

PEACH-FACED LOVEBIRDS sometimes have a phobia of human hands. Even hand-fed babies who otherwise love their humans can have this phobia. If you keep forcing your hands on a bird who obviously fears the human hand, you could harm your relationship with your pet.

I always offer these phobic birds the choice of a stick or my arm instead of a hand. Keep up the stick training. Work with your pet every day. I cannot explain why a bird that fears a hand will happily hop onto my arm and then run up to snuggle on my shoulder, but I've seen it enough to know that phobias are irrational.

Work with your bird to create a positive experience each time your pet plays with you.

My bird is terrorizing me, my kids, or my other pets.

IF YOUR LOVEBIRD IS flying at your head and slapping you with its wings, you have gone too long between wing trims. This behavior usually vanishes in a flash when the primary feathers are kept properly trimmed.

My bird won't stop shrieking.

YOU HAVE TO IDENTIFY the cause of the shrieking. An isolated bird will call constantly in an attempt to make contact. If you respond to these calls, you have provided your pet with the response it was seeking. On the other hand, if you don't respond, your bird may shriek louder and louder to demand your attention.

As we've said before, pair-bond birds like lovebirds shouldn't be isolated. Make sure your bird has a place in your home or wherever else you travel that allows your pet to observe you and feel involved in your day-to-day activities. A single pet lovebird can be a devoted pet indeed, but if you don't have the time to return that constant devotion, you might do better to pair up your lovebird with a companion.

Aviary pairs do make some noise, although I haven't found it to be particularly loud, unpleasant, or prolonged. Some pairs will sound off at dawn, because they can hear the so-called "dawn chorus" outside. As you have probably noticed, many small birds sing around sunrise, and your lovebirds may wish to join in. This is perfectly natural. Expecting your birds to be completely silent isn't realistic.

However, if your birds are shrieking for an unusual length of time or at an unusual hour, you should investigate. Something is wrong.

On occasion, a perfectly happy solo lovebird may start shrieking back and forth to a bird or another source of noise it can hear outside. Handle this by playing soft music or turning on a fan to mask the noise coming from outdoors.

My Lovebird Is Plucking Out Its Feathers

LOVEBIRDS, LIKE MOST other parrots, can develop a disorder where they begin to compulsively pluck out their own feathers. Naturally, this is upsetting, especially in a pet you have specifically chosen for the beauty of its plumage.

Consult with an avian vet as soon as possible. There are many treatable causes for this problem, such as a hormone imbalance or red mites. If you treat the problem fast enough, you can prevent your lovebird from developing a bad habit of feather-plucking.

Unfortunately, we don't know the cause or the cure for every case of feather-plucking. Some happy lovebirds with a clean bill of health continue to pluck. Make sure your lovebird continues to enjoy plenty of attention, toys, and exercise. Even if you can't eliminate the self-plucking behavior, you can help reduce it.

My Lovebird Is Laying Eggs

A FEMALE LOVEBIRD MAY lay eggs even if she doesn't have a mate. The eggs will be infertile, but each egg produced removes vitamins and minerals from her body, so you want to discourage her from laying more eggs if at all possible.

In the wild, if a predator removed the eggs, or if she accidentally broke a clear egg, she would keep laying to replace them. Some pet birds, including peach-faced lovebirds, can be trapped in a cycle of laying eggs over and over again, until her body is depleted of nutrients.

Calcium— the same mineral that builds strong bones— is required to build strong eggshells. Therefore, if your bird lays too many eggs, her body can be depleted of calcium, which can cause multiple serious health problems, including egg binding. As the name suggests, egg binding occurs when the egg gets stuck in your bird's cloaca. Unfortunately, this condition can lead to sudden death. Prevention is always better than treatment in such a case.

Therefore, once their lovebird starts laying, many people remove the real eggs and replace them with unbreakable lookalike plastic eggs. If you simply remove the real eggs, the lovebird's body will be triggered to replace them. However, if you replace the real ones with fakes, the lovebird's body will usually turn off the desire to lay and move forward with the desire to sit on the brood. After a couple of weeks or so, she will get bored with the project when the eggs fail to hatch. With any luck, the desire to lay will have passed for another season.

If your lovebird won't stop laying eggs, she is at risk of dying suddenly from egg-binding or a vitamin deficiency. Consult with your avian vet as soon as possible. Hormone shots are one possible treatment that could save your bird's life.

My Lovebird Lost Her Tameness

LIFE GOT IN THE WAY, and you didn't spend as much time as you needed to with your personal pet. Now she is no longer tame and isn't interested in a relationship with you. All is not lost.

You have two choices. Work with the bird more often, several times a day, every day. Keep the bird with you on a playpen or even in a portable cage so it is never alone.

However, it is entirely possible that you simply don't have the time to invest in working with your bird right now. In that case, be realistic about how you can keep your bird happy and healthy. Lovebirds don't tolerate "alone" time or "me" time very well. They are designed by nature to go two by two.

Consider getting a second bird (as well as a second cage or flight). Introduce the birds a bit at a time, either by putting their cages close together or by allowing them to hang out together on a playpen. Eventually, you can move them together into a third cage.

I never advise using the original cage of either bird to house the new buddies. Because lovebirds are so territorial by nature, it's possible the original cage owner would feel driven to harm the newcomer. Place them together on ground that is new to both of them. And supervise the situation carefully until you are confident they're getting along.

A Beginner's Guide to Breeding

WE WON'T TALK ABOUT how to breed the rare species here. That is a game for the advanced hobbyist who has already gained serious experience working with the classic colony-breeding lovebirds— the peach-faced lovebird and the four eye-ring species.

It follows that your first decision will be whether to breed your lovebirds in cages or in a large colony. If you are planning to breed certain color mutations or to pair certain birds, the choice is made for you. You will need to breed in cages, with each pair given its own secure cage where it can rule the roost on its own territory.

If you prefer to breed in a colony aviary, you need to make sure you have enough birds, enough space, and enough nest boxes. Lovebirds are monogamous birds with a powerful sense of territory. You should have either a single pair per enclosure, or you should have "many." Lovebirds can count and create a dangerous pecking order when you have too few birds in a colony. To set up an aviary with three, four, or five lovebirds in it is almost certainly a mistake. An alpha pair will form, which will turn on the lesser-ranked birds and attempt to drive them off the territory. Since they can't escape your aviary, the alpha pair can be enraged to the point where they kill first the weakest bird, then the next weakest, and so on.

Think long and hard before you choose to set up an aviary. Can you provide sufficient space and care for a larger number of birds? If so, you can set up a beautiful flight that provides you with a great deal of visual and emotional satisfaction. You will have a front-row seat for their colorful lives, but your birds won't be tightly bonded to you. They will be deeply involved in their own social structure. Your emotional satisfaction will be closer to the pleasure the tropical fish hobbyists take from their tanks— the pleasure of creating and observing a world of beauty.

Just like the tropical fish hobbyist, you will need to keep a watchful eye on your charges to monitor their health and also to put a stop to any bullying. Otherwise, the lovebird colony has some pros and cons when compared to the fish-keeping hobby.

*A colony of lovebirds will be noisier.

*Keeping their environment clean is easier and more intuitive than keeping a tropical fish tank clean, healthy, and well-balanced.

Two other points to consider:

*After your lovebirds have paired off in the aviary, you will need to remove any oddball or bullied birds. Do you have an appropriate space to care for your so-called leftovers?

*A walk-in aviary should have a double door (also known as an airlock) system. You should always close the outer door before you open the inner door. Otherwise, you may lose some of your flock to the great outdoors.

Many, if not most hobbyists and virtually all exhibitors, prefer to breed their lovebirds in cages— one pair, and only one pair, to each breeding cage. In this way, breeders can control who mates with who, allowing them to create the color mutations of their choice.

Of course, your control in these matters is not one hundred percent. You must observe carefully when you pair your birds to make sure the lovebirds are accepting their mates. It can happen that two lovebirds find a way to quarrel rather than to bond. In that case, you must act quickly to separate the incompatible birds before one of them hurts or kills the other. Lovebirds are aggressive, and they don't tolerate intruders on their territory. If the mate you picked is viewed as an intruder, you have trouble.

Before Breeding Season

YOUR FIRST STEP IS to make sure you have true pairs. This may be easy enough to accomplish in a colony where the birds pick their own mates, but it may be less easy if you only have two birds in a breeding cage. Since males and females of the popular species look much alike, you will probably want to DNA test your birds to make sure you have a true pair.

Of course, if the "pair" is already acting coupled up, you may be tempted to go ahead and make some assumptions. Keep in mind, if there is only one potential mate available, lovebirds can be adaptable. If your untested birds get busy snuggling and then end up laying eight or more eggs in their cozy nest box, guess what. The odds are decent that you have two females producing infertile eggs. Two males can also happily play house, although you will never observe any eggs in that case.

If your heart is set on breeding, this author strongly urges you to get your lovebirds DNA-tested to be sure. Follow the instructions from your vet or lab to collect the feathers required for the test.

A vet check might be in order anyway before you start the project. Females, in particular, can put their own lives at risk by starting too young or by laying too often. You always want to begin your breeding projects with strong, fully adult birds. Don't provide nest boxes, nesting material, or special foods that encourage breeding until you are confident your birds are old enough— at least a year old and perhaps a bit more.

Once you have the go-ahead to breed your birds, you will want to supply the following items:

*The right nest box— Like most parrots, lovebirds are cavity nesters in the wild. The popular species happily accept commercial or homemade wooden nestboxes as a substitute. Breeders have successfully used nest boxes labeled for cockatiels and budgies as well as lovebirds.

An aviary should have at least one more nest box than you have pairs. For cage breeding, I prefer the use of external nest boxes attached to the outside of the cage, rather than internal boxes stuffed inside the cage. Choose or build in an access window that allows you to check the nest without stuffing your hands in the cage.

Remember, lovebirds tend to dislike intrusive hands. And they truly dislike home invasions of their personal territory.

*Nesting material— Unlike most parrots, and more like finches, the popular lovebirds like to build their own nest inside the cavity. That means you need to supply plenty of their favorite material to forestall the birds from picking their own or their partner's feathers.

Lovebirds can be a lot of fun to watch during this process of construction. Female peach-faced lovebirds in particular love to shred their materials into long ribbons that they stuff into their tails to fly over to the nest cavity. They will shred recycled books, magazines, and documents all day long, but you can make them very happy by offering more natural materials like palm fronds, willows, and mulberry branches, as well as commercial nesting material sold by bird and pet suppliers.

The eye-ring species may fetch and carry with their bills, but they still put on a good show. Instead of building the open-cup nest of the peach-faced, they create intricate structures complete with a domed roof overhead. The entire nest box may look as if it is crammed full of the material to the overflow point.

*An especially rich diet that includes fresh greens, sweet corn, and any other fresh fruit and vegetables your lovebirds can be coaxed to eat alongside their usual seed and/or pellet-based diet. Each pair should also have free access to a clean mineral block. Creating eggs takes a lot of nutrients out of a female lovebird's body. If the birds refuse to eat an ideal diet, you would be wise to consult with your avian vet or more advanced breeders in your local club to get hands-on advice about the best supplements to support your breeder lovebirds' health.

*Wild lovebirds are stimulated to breed by the coming of the rainy season. Consider playing a recording of rain falling to stimulate your pair to get going.

A Word of Caution

BREEDING LOVEBIRDS shouldn't be considered a "set it and forget it" exercise. Monitor your birds carefully, particularly the female. If she is straining to lay or is sitting on the floor with a swollen vent or showing any other signs of visible distress, she may be suffering from egg-binding— a life-threatening medical emergency. Get her to a vet as soon as possible. This is such a common problem with lovebirds that you may want to defer attempting to breed your birds until you have located a competent avian vet in your area. An emergency could come at you fast.

A Quick Note About Hand-feeding

IF YOU'RE BREEDING your lovebirds for personal pocket pets, you will want to hand-feed your babies. Lovebirds who haven't been hand-fed almost never bond to their human instead of another lovebird.

Hand-fed babies can make superior pets because they have grown up from an early age accepting humans as a source of food. However, if you think back to the chapter on choosing a baby lovebird, you'll remember that we talked about the challenges beginners face when they attempt to hand-feed small parrots.

Hand-feeding demands a careful touch. You won't pick up the proper technique from reading a book. This author strongly advises you to find a way to learn under the watchful eyes of a more experienced breeder. An experienced guide willing to supervise the first few times you hand-feed is absolutely worth their weight in pirate's gold.

That said, you will also find it helpful to study some of the hand-feeding videos you find on YouTube or elsewhere on the internet. These videos have the advantage that you can slow them down to watch them several times to study some of the fine points.

However, even the best video isn't a substitute for someone there at your side to give you a hands-on demonstration. Join a local club, or volunteer at a rescue. Do whatever it takes to network with people willing to share their knowledge for the benefit of the birds.

Just How Smart Are Lovebirds?

THE ANSWER IS, "VERY." Like many smaller birds, they are aggressive all out of proportions to their size. As a result, people often misunderstand lovebirds. They may even assume they're not all that smart— that they are the classic birdbrains who run around being fueled by their hormones.

Lovebirds do have many instinctive behaviors. However, if you start with patience, determination, and some basic understanding of their psychology, you can do some amazing things. I strongly recommend that all lovebird fanciers watch a free copy of **Bill and**

Coo, a 1948 movie that is currently in the Public Domain and available for free download from the Internet Archive at:

https://archive.org/details/Bill_and_Coo

At the time of writing, this film could also be found on YouTube, where we trust it will be allowed to remain as a Public Domain film and a piece of history.

Other than the prologue, all of the parts are played by animals, mostly birds, a surprising number of them lovebirds, including the two romantic leads, Bill and Coo. No animatronics. No robots. No CGI. This film is made with real lovebirds, and they performed beautifully.

The feat is all the more remarkable because this film was made before the days when baby lovebirds were hand-fed to make them more trusting of humans and easier to handle. Patience, love, understanding, and more patience are the keys to caring for and training your dream lovebird.

Today, we have a headstart because we usually begin with a hand-fed baby lovebird who trusts us. If you can devote the time to keeping your lovebird tame and friendly, you will have a spunky pocket pet who provides hours of entertainment for many years.

If you want a more laid-back relationship where you observe your birds interacting with each other, you can have that too. Few hobbies bring as much beauty and life to your home as the well-kept lovebird aviary.

♪♪♪

If you enjoyed this book, please return to the retailer where you bought it to leave your review. A five-star review is a great encouragement to a new author.

Still not sure a lovebird is right for you? Consider the cockatiel, the subject of my new book, **Your Dream Pet Cockatiel: Twenty-first Century Care, Feeding, Training, and Breeding Strategies.**

About the Author

DARLA BIRDE IS THE pen name of the owner of a small bird rescue that does not re-sell the birds in her care. She has worked with lovebirds, cockatiels, budgerigars, and many other birds for over a decade.

Printed in Great Britain
by Amazon